My First Picture Dictionary

William A. Jenkins
Andrew Schiller

Scott, Foresman and Company
Editorial Offices: Glenview, Illinois

Regional Offices:
Palo Alto, California •
Tucker, Georgia • Glenview, Illinois •
Oakland, New Jersey • Dallas, Texas

Contents

ISBN 0-673-12422-3   ISBN 0-673-12423-1   45678910-WAK-90898887868584

Copyright © 1982, 1975, 1970
Scott, Foresman and Company, Glenview, Illinois
All Rights Reserved. Printed in the United States of America.

ABC
DEFG
HIJK
LMNOP
QRSTUV
WXYZ

4

abc defg hijk lmnop qrstuv wxyz

Words That Name People

artist   artists

An artist paints pictures. Museums have pictures painted by artists.

astronaut   astronauts

An astronaut rides in a spaceship. Astronauts landed on the moon.

aunt   aunts

An aunt is a relative. Penny and Paul have two aunts, Aunt Ruth and Aunt Alice. See the picture for family on page 12.

baby   babies

A baby is a very young child. Little babies can't walk.

Words That Name People

baker   bakers

A baker makes bread and other things to eat. Bakers work in bakeries.

barber   barbers

A barber cuts hair. Barbers work in a barber shop.

boy   boys

A boy grows up to be a man. Boys grow up to be men.

bride   brides

A bride is a woman who is getting married.

bridegroom   bridegrooms

A bridegroom is a man who is getting married.

7

Words That Name People

brother   brothers

A brother is a relative. Paul is Penny's brother. See the picture for family on page 12.

carpenter   carpenters

A carpenter builds houses out of wood.

checker   checkers

A checker checks the things you buy in a supermarket.

child   children

A child is a young boy or a young girl. Children grow up to be men and women.

Words That Name People

class   classes

A class is a group of pupils. Some classes have many pupils.

clown   clowns

A clown makes people laugh. Clowns wear funny clothes.

cook   cooks

A cook knows how to cook food. Cooks prepare meals.

cousin   cousins

A cousin is a relative. Penny and Paul have four cousins, Peter, Tim, Jane, and Sue. See the picture for family on page 12.

cowboy   cowboys
cowgirl   cowgirls

A cowboy and a cowgirl work on a ranch. Cowboys and cowgirls often ride horses.

Words That Name People

custodian   custodians

A custodian takes care of a building. Most schools have custodians.

dad   dads

Dad is a short name for father.

daughter   daughters

A daughter is a relative. Penny is the daughter of her father and mother. See the picture for family on page 12.

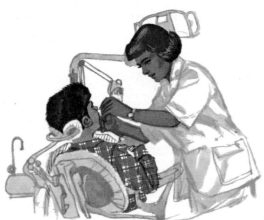

dentist   dentists

A dentist cleans and takes care of a person's teeth.

Words That Name People

diver   divers

A diver can swim under water.
Divers strap tanks of air on
their backs.

doctor   doctors

A doctor takes care of sick people.

driver   drivers

A driver is a person who makes a
car or truck or bus move.

druggist   druggists

A druggist works in a drugstore.
You buy medicine from a druggist.

electrician   electricians

An electrician fixes lights.

family   families

Parents and their children
are a family. All the
people in a family are
relatives.

Grandfather and Grandmother Smith

Uncle Bob
Smith

Aunt Alice and Uncle Jim Smith

Cousin Peter Smith

Penny Baker

Paul Baker

Words That Name People

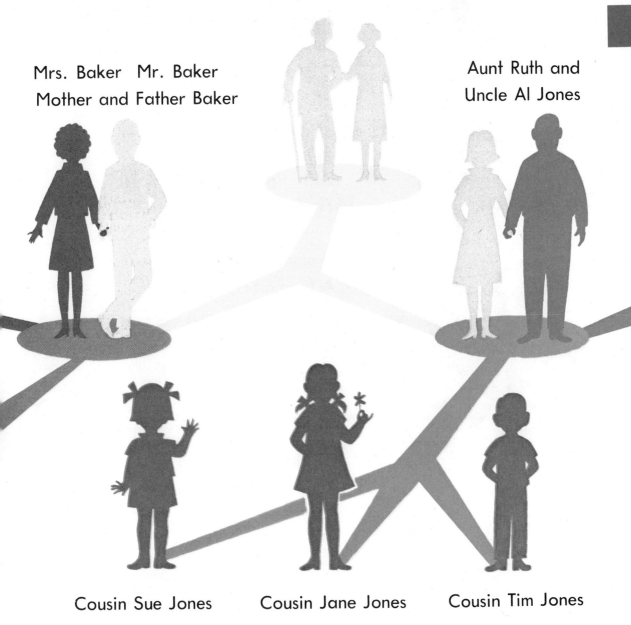

Grandfather and Grandmother Baker

Mrs. Baker Mr. Baker
Mother and Father Baker

Aunt Ruth and
Uncle Al Jones

Cousin Sue Jones   Cousin Jane Jones   Cousin Tim Jones

Words That Name People

father   fathers
A father is a relative. Paul's
father is one of his parents. See
the picture for family on page 12.

firefighter   firefighters
A firefighter puts out fires.
Firefighters ride on fire trucks.

fireman   firemen
A fireman is a firefighter.

friend   friends
A friend is someone who likes you.
You may have many friends.

girl   girls
A girl grows up to be a woman.
Girls grow up to be women.

Words That Name People

grandchild   grandchildren

A grandchild is a relative.
Grandmother and Grandfather
Baker have five grandchildren. See
the picture for family on page 12.

granddaughter   granddaughters

A granddaughter is a relative.
Penny is a granddaughter of
Grandmother and Grandfather
Baker. See the picture for family
on page 12.

grandfather   grandfathers
grandpa   grandpas

A grandfather is a relative. Paul
and Penny have two grandfathers.
See the picture for family on
page 12.

grandmother   grandmothers
grandma   grandmas

A grandmother is a relative. Paul
and Penny have two grandmothers.
See the picture for family on
page 12.

15

Words That Name People

grandson   grandsons

A grandson is a relative. Paul
is a grandson of Grandmother and
Grandfather Baker. See the
picture for family on page 12.

guard   guards

A guard takes care of people or
things. Guards help children
cross the street.

gymnast   gymnasts

A gymnast does many hard exercises.
Gymnasts must be strong.

janitor   janitors

A janitor takes care of a building.
Janitors are custodians.

judge   judges

A judge often has to decide who
is right and who is wrong.

Words That Name People

librarian   librarians

A librarian works in a library. Librarians help you find good books to read.

lifeguard   lifeguards

A lifeguard works at a beach or a pool. Lifeguards guard people who are in the water.

magician   magicians

A magician can do magic tricks. Magicians are fun to watch.

mail carrier   mail carriers

The mail carrier delivers mail. Mail carriers bring letters from the post office.

mailman   mailmen

A mailman is a mail carrier.

Words That Name People

mama   mamas

Mama is a short name for mother.

man   men

A boy grows up to be a man. Boys grow up to be men.

mayor   mayors

Ms. Fox is our mayor.
Mayors work for towns and cities.

mechanic   mechanics

A mechanic fixes engines. Some mechanics work in garages.

mom   moms

Mom is another name for mother.

Words That Name People

mother mothers

A mother is a relative. Paul's mother is one of his parents. See the picture for family on page 12.

neighbor neighbors

A neighbor lives near you. Our neighbors are working in their yard, too.

nephew nephews

A nephew is a relative. Paul is Uncle Al and Aunt Ruth's nephew. See the picture for family on page 12.

niece nieces

A niece is a relative. Penny is Uncle Al and Aunt Ruth's niece. See the picture for family on page 12.

Words That Name People

nurse   nurses

A nurse takes care of sick people.
Some nurses visit homes.

operator   operators

An operator makes something work.
Telephone operators can help you
dial a number.

painter   painters

A painter paints the inside and
outside of houses.

papa   papas

Papa is a short name for father.

parent   parents

A parent is a mother or father. Paul's
parents are his mother and father.
See the picture for family on page 12.

Words That Name People

people
Men, women, children, and babies are people.

person   **persons**
A person is any boy, girl, man, or woman. Each one of the people in this picture is a person.

photographer   **photographers**
A photographer takes pictures. Photographers often work for newspapers.

Pilgrim   **Pilgrims**
A Pilgrim had to hunt for food. Pilgrims came to live in America long ago.

Words That Name People

pilot   pilots

A pilot flies an airplane or
steers a ship.

plumber   plumbers

A plumber fixes broken water
pipes in houses.

police officer   police officers

A police officer protects people.
A policeman and a policewoman are
police officers.

postman   postmen

A postman is a mail carrier.

principal   principals

A principal is the person in charge
of a school. The principal visited
our class.

Words That Name People

relative   relatives

A relative is someone who belongs to your family. All the Bakers and Smiths and Joneses are relatives of Penny and Paul. See the picture for family on page 12.

reporter   reporters

A reporter looks for news. Reporters find out what is happening and write about it.

salesperson   salespersons

A salesperson is someone who sells things.

sister   sisters

A sister is a relative. Penny is Paul's sister. See the picture for family on page 12.

son   sons

A son is a relative. Paul is the son of his father and mother. See the picture for family on page 12.

23

Words That Name People

superintendent   superintendents

The superintendent of schools
is speaking on TV today.

teacher   teachers

A teacher helps people learn.
Teachers work in schools.

twin   twins

Twins are two persons born at the
same time, to the same parents.
Penny and Paul are twins. See the
picture for family on page 12.

typist   typists

A typist operates a typewriter.
Many typists work in a big office.

Words That Name People

uncle   uncles

An uncle is a relative. Paul has
three uncles, Uncle Al, Uncle Bob,
and Uncle Jim. See the picture
for family on page 12.

waiter   waiters

A waiter is a man who serves food
in a restaurant.

waitress   waitresses

A waitress is a woman who serves
food in a restaurant.

watchman   watchmen

A watchman guards a building.
Most watchmen work at night.

woman   women

A girl grows up to be a woman.
Girls grow up to be women.

Words That Name Animals

alligator alligators

An alligator lives near water.
Alligators have thick skin.

animal animals

Dogs and cats, lions and tigers,
are animals. Birds and fish and
insects are animals, too.

ant ants

An ant is a small insect that lives
in the ground. Ants work hard.

bat bats

A bat looks like a mouse with
wings. Bats can fly.

bear bears

A bear is a huge animal that likes
honey. Bears sleep all winter.

Words That Name Animals

beaver   beavers

A beaver has sharp teeth and a flat tail. Beavers can cut down a tree with their teeth.

bee   bees

A bee is an insect that makes honey and wax. Bees can fly.

beetle   beetles

A beetle is an insect. Beetles have hard covers on their wings.

bird   birds

A bird is an animal that has feathers and wings. Most birds can fly.

bluebird   bluebirds

A bluebird is a small bird. Bluebirds sing songs.

Words That Name Animals

bug   bugs

A bug is an insect. Bugs crawl.

butterfly   butterflies

A butterfly is an insect with
large, brightly colored wings.
Some butterflies only live one day.

calf   calves

A calf is a cow's baby. Calves
run and jump.

camel   camels

A camel can carry a heavy load.
Camels live in the desert. Some
camels have two humps.

canary   canaries

A canary is a small yellow bird
that sings. Many people keep
canaries in cages.

Words That Name Animals

cardinal   cardinals

A cardinal is a bright-red bird.

cat   cats

A cat has soft fur. Cats make good pets.

caterpillar   caterpillars

A caterpillar looks like a fuzzy worm. It turns into a butterfly.

cattle

Cows, bulls, and steers are cattle.

chicken   chickens

A chicken is a bird raised for food. Chicken is good to eat.

chipmunk   chipmunks

A chipmunk looks like a small squirrel. Chipmunks have stripes.

Words That Name Animals

colt   colts

A colt is a young horse or donkey.
Colts like to run and jump.

cow   cows

A cow is a farm animal. Cows give
milk. Most cows are gentle.

crow   crows

A crow is a large, shiny black
bird with a loud cry.

cub   cubs

A cub is a baby animal. Baby
bears and baby lions are cubs.

deer   deer

A deer is a wild animal. Many
deer have antlers.

Words That Name Animals

dinosaur   dinosaurs

There is no dinosaur alive today.
Dinosaurs were huge animals that
lived many, many years ago.

dog   dogs

A dog is a good pet.

dolphin   dolphins

A dolphin is a sea animal. It
looks like a large fish. Dolphins
can do tricks.

donkey   donkeys

A donkey is smaller than a horse.
Donkeys can carry heavy loads.

duck   ducks
duckling   ducklings

A duck is a bird that swims and
flies. Some ducks are wild. A
duckling is a baby duck. Ducklings
can swim like ducks.

Words That Name Animals

eagle   eagles

An eagle is a large, strong bird.
It builds its nest in a high place.

elephant   elephants

An elephant is a very large animal
with a trunk.

fish   fish

A fish is an animal that lives in
water. Fish have fins instead of
legs or wings.

fly   flies

A fly is an insect with wings.
Flies buzz when they fly.

foal   foals

A foal is a baby horse.

Words That Name Animals

fox   foxes

A fox looks like a small dog.
Foxes are wild animals.

frog   frogs

A frog has smooth skin and no tail.
Frogs live in or near water.

gerbil   gerbils

A gerbil looks like a small mouse.
Gerbils make good pets.

giraffe   giraffes

A giraffe has a long neck.
Giraffes are tallest of all the
animals.

goat   goats

A goat has horns and a short tail.
Some people drink goat's milk.

Words That Name Animals

goldfish   goldfish

A goldfish is a small, brightly colored fish. Goldfish often live in glass bowls.

goose   geese

A goose is a bird that swims. Geese are larger than ducks.

guppy   guppies

A guppy is a very small fish. Some people raise guppies.

hamster   hamsters

A hamster is like a mouse, but it is larger. Hamsters are sometimes kept as pets.

hen   hens

A hen is a female chicken. Hens lay eggs.

Words That Name Animals

hippopotamus   hippopotamuses
A hippopotamus is a large animal with thick skin. It has short legs and a big head. It likes to swim.

horse   horses
A horse can carry a person or pull a wagon. Some horses do tricks.

hummingbird   hummingbirds
A hummingbird is tiny. Its wings move so fast they hum.

insect   insects
An insect is any small animal with six legs. Flies and bees are insects.

kangaroo   kangaroos
A kangaroo has a thick, strong tail. The female kangaroo carries her baby in a pouch.

35

Words That Name Animals

kid   kids

A kid is a baby goat.

kitten   kittens

A kitten is a baby cat.

koala   koalas

A koala looks like a little bear.
Koalas live in trees.

ladybug   ladybugs

A ladybug is small and round.
Ladybugs have black spots.

lamb   lambs

A lamb is a baby sheep.

leopard   leopards

A leopard is a big, wild cat.
Leopards have spots.

Words That Name Animals

lion   lions

A lion is a large, strong animal.
It has a loud roar.

lizard   lizards

A lizard has short legs and a
long tail.

monkey   monkeys

A monkey is very smart. It is
fun to watch monkeys at the zoo.

mosquito   mosquitoes

A mosquito is an insect that flies.
Mosquitoes bite people.

mouse   mice

A mouse is a small animal with a
long tail. People don't want mice
in their houses.

Words That Name Animals

opossum   opossums

An opossum carries its babies on its back. Opossums live in trees.

owl   owls

An owl is a bird with large eyes. It can see well in the dark.

panda   pandas

A panda looks like a bear. It is black and white.

parakeet   parakeets

A parakeet is a small bird. Some parakeets can say words.

parrot   parrots

A parrot is a large bird with bright-colored feathers. Some parrots can talk.

Words That Name Animals

peacock   peacocks

A peacock is a big bird. Its tail feathers spread out like a huge fan.

penguin   penguins

A penguin is a bird that swims but cannot fly. Penguins live near the South Pole.

pet   pets

A pet is an animal kept and treated with love. Liu has two pets.

pig   pigs

A pig is raised for its meat. Bacon and ham come from pigs.

pigeon   pigeons

A pigeon is a bird with short legs. Many pigeons live in the city. People often go to the park and feed pigeons.

Words That Name Animals

pony   ponies

A pony is a kind of small horse. Ponies are fun to ride.

porcupine   porcupines

A porcupine is covered with stiff, sharp quills. The quills keep other animals away.

puppy   puppies

A puppy is a baby dog. Puppies like to play.

rabbit   rabbits

A rabbit has soft fur and long ears. Rabbits are good pets.

raccoon   raccoons

A raccoon looks as if it is wearing a black mask.

Words That Name Animals

rat   rats

A rat looks like a mouse, but it is larger.

reindeer   reindeer

A reindeer is a kind of large deer. Reindeer live where it is cold.

rhinoceros   rhinoceroses

A rhinoceros has one or two horns on its nose. It is a wild animal.

robin   robins

A robin is a bird with a red breast. Robins eat worms.

rooster   roosters

A rooster is a male chicken. Roosters crow in the morning.

Words That Name Animals

seal   seals

A seal lives in or near cold water. Seals in a circus can do tricks.

sheep   sheep

A sheep has a thick coat of wool. Sheep are raised on ranches and farms.

skunk   skunks

A skunk is black. It has white stripes down its back.

snail   snails

A snail is a tiny animal with a shell but no legs. It always moves very slowly.

snake   snakes

A snake is long and thin. It has no legs. It crawls on the ground.

Words That Name Animals

sparrow   sparrows

A sparrow is a small bird.
Sparrows are brown and gray.

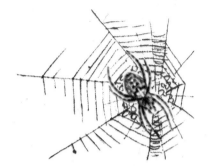

spider   spiders

A spider has eight long legs and
no wings. Spiders spin webs.

squirrel   squirrels

A squirrel has a big bushy tail.
Squirrels live in trees and eat nuts.

starfish   starfish

A starfish is a sea animal that
looks like a star. Starfish are
often found on the beach.

swan   swans

A swan is a large white bird with
a long, thin neck. It lives near
the water and likes to swim.

Words That Name Animals

tiger   tigers

A tiger looks like a big cat, but
it is wild. It has stripes.

toad   toads

A toad looks like a brown frog.
Toads often live in gardens or
yards. Toads are hard to see.

turkey   turkeys

A turkey is a large bird. Turkeys
are raised for food.

turtle   turtles

A turtle has four legs and a hard
shell. Many turtles live in or
near water.

whale   whales

A whale is a sea animal. It looks
like a huge fish.

Words That Name Animals

wolf   wolves

A wolf is a wild animal that looks like a dog. Wolves howl.

woodpecker   woodpeckers

A woodpecker is a bird with a strong bill. It can peck holes in trees.

worm   worms

A worm is a small, thin animal without legs. It lives in the ground. Birds and fish eat worms.

zebra   zebras

A zebra is a wild animal. It looks like a striped horse.

45

Words That Name
Storybook Characters

brownie   brownies

A brownie looks like a tiny person.
Brownies help people when no one
is looking.

dragon   dragons

A dragon is a huge monster.
Dragons breathe fire.

dwarf   dwarfs

A dwarf looks like a little person.
Dwarfs have magic power.

elf   elves

An elf looks like a tiny person.
Elves are full of tricks.

fairy   fairies

A fairy looks like a tiny person.
Fairies have magic power.

Words That Name Storybook Characters

ghost   ghosts

A ghost is a shadowy white figure.

giant   giants

A giant looks like a huge person.
Giants are very strong.

goblin   goblins

A goblin looks like an ugly-looking
little man or animal.

Jack Frost

Jack Frost paints leaves in the
fall. Nobody ever sees him.

king   kings

A king is a man who rules a
country. Kings wear crowns.

Words That Name Storybook Characters

knight   knights

A knight is a man who does good deeds. Knights wear armor.

ogre   ogres

An ogre is a horrible monster that eats people.

pirate   pirates

A pirate is a bad person who steals ships and buries treasure.

prince   princes

A prince is a king's son. In stories many princes are handsome.

princess   princesses

A princess is a king's daughter. In stories most princesses are beautiful.

Words That Name Storybook Characters

queen   queens

In stories a queen is a king's wife. Queens wear crowns.

troll   trolls

A troll is a funny-looking creature. Trolls live in caves.

unicorn   unicorns

A unicorn looks like a horse. It has a long horn on its forehead. Unicorns are white.

witch   witches

A witch looks like an old woman. She rides a broom. Witches are mean.

wizard   wizards

A wizard looks like a man. He has magic power. Some wizards are good. Some are bad.

Action Words

answer

Bobby is answering the telephone.
He answered it as soon as it rang.

ask

Lia is asking her dad a question.
She asked him to read her a story.

bake

Dad and Johnny are baking cookies.
They baked a cake, too.

bark

Max is barking loudly. He barked
at the cat.

Action Words

begin

Snow is beginning to fall. It began all of a sudden. The wind has begun to blow, too.

bite

George was biting an apple. He bit his finger by mistake. He has bitten two fingers.

blow

Jim is blowing his horn. Pam blew her horn first. All the children have blown their horns.

boast

Tom is boasting about his grades in school. He boasted that he is very smart.

Action Words

break

Bruce was breaking an egg into a
pan. It broke on the floor instead.
He has broken two eggs so far.

brush

Jane is brushing her hair again.
She brushed it this morning.

build

Dave is building a castle. He
built a house yesterday. He has
built a whole city.

button

Jean is buttoning her coat. She
buttoned her sweater first.

Action Words

buy

Mother is buying a car. She bought a red car last year. She has never bought a blue one.

call

Jenny is calling her grandmother. She called her on the telephone.

carry

The cat is carrying her kitten home. She carried it across the street.

catch

Jessie is catching the ball. She caught the ball in her mitt. She has caught it every time.

Action Words

choose

Sally is choosing a book. She chose two stories. She has chosen a picture book, too.

chug

The train is chugging up the hill. It chugged to the top of the hill.

churn

The wheel is churning in the mud. It churned in the hole.

climb

The cat is climbing the ladder. It climbed a tree yesterday.

Action Words

close

Rose is closing the window. She closed it to keep out the wind.

color

She is coloring with crayons. She colored the flowers yellow.

comb

Tom is combing his hair. Joe combed his hair long ago.

come

The train is coming. It came out of the tunnel and stopped. It has come over the hill slowly.

Action Words

cry

The puppy is still crying. The puppy cried all night.

cut

Uncle Lee is cutting meat. He cut a big piece of meat for me. He has cut one for you, too.

dance

The girls are dancing at Joy's house. They danced fast.

dial

Barbara is dialing May's number. She dialed the wrong number first.

Action Words

dig

The dog is digging a hole. It dug two holes yesterday. It has dug holes all over the yard.

dive

Sam is diving into the pool. He dived off the board.

do

What is Grandpa doing in the kitchen? He does the dishes. He did the cooking. He has done all the work.

draw

Ruth is drawing a picture. She drew a house. Now she has drawn two trees.

Action Words

dress

Carl is dressing for school. He dressed all by himself.

drink

Lois is drinking another glass of milk. She drank milk for breakfast. She had drunk two glasses of milk for lunch.

drive

Mother is driving the car. She drove out of the garage. She has driven to work.

drop

Peg is dropping a letter in the mailbox. She dropped it on the ground first.

Action Words

dump

The baby is dumping his toys. He dumped toys everywhere.

eat

The Martínez family is eating supper. Rosa ate everything on her plate. She could have eaten more.

erase

The teacher is erasing the chalkboard. She erased the poem.

fall

The leaves are falling from the trees. Many leaves fell when the wind blew. Most of the leaves have fallen since yesterday.

Action Words

feed

Carmen is feeding the chickens.
She fed them after school. She
has fed them twice today.

fight

The kids are fighting. They fought
over the ball. They have fought
every time they played ball.

fill

Mr. Simmons is filling the glass.
He filled it with fruit juice.

find

Danny is finding four-leaf clovers
everywhere he looks. He found
three in the yard. He has found
ten today.

Action Words

fish

The people are still fishing.
They fished all day.

fix

Dad is fixing the car. We both
fixed my bicycle.

fold

Mom and Dad are folding towels.
Dad took them out of the dryer.

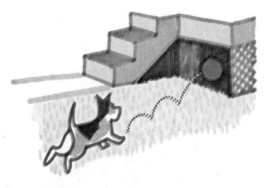

follow

The dog was following the ball. He
followed it under the porch.

Action Words

forget

Are you forgetting anything? One girl forgot her mittens. I have forgotten my scarf.

gasp

Jay is gasping for breath. He gasped for air after the race.

get

Mrs. Roddy is getting the mail. She got it out of the mailbox. She has gotten many letters.

give

Mother is giving me a birthday present. She gave my sister one last month. She has given my brother his present.

Action Words

go

Roger is going to the store. He goes there every day. He went there yesterday. He has gone twice today.

grow

The sunflower is growing fast. It grew more last night. It has grown every day.

guess

Larry is guessing the number of jelly beans. He guessed there are 900 jelly beans.

hammer

The woman is hammering a nail. She hammered three nails.

63

Action Words

help

Patsy is helping her mother.
She helped paint the wall.

hide

The kitten is hiding behind the chair. It hid there before. It has hidden in the closet, too.

hit

Joe is not hitting the ball.
Once he hit it across the street.
Today he has not hit it at all.

hold

Cindy is holding her dog. She held the dog in her arms.

Action Words

hurt

Mark's arm hurts. He hurt it playing football.

iron

Mother is ironing clothes. She ironed four dresses after work.

jump

Nancy is jumping up and down. She jumped over the flowers.

keep

Can you keep a secret? Joy kept many secrets.

kick

George was kicking his ball. He kicked it into a tree.

Action Words

know

Do you know that boy? I knew his sister in kindergarten. I have never known his name.

laugh

The boy was laughing at the clown. He laughed very hard.

live

Kay lives in the country. She once lived in the city.

look

Jim is looking for a pencil. He looked, but didn't find one.

lose

Did you lose something? Luis lost one shoe.

make

Sue is making pancakes. She and Moy made breakfast.

Action Words

milk

The farmer is milking the brown cow. He milked the other cows.

miss

Don't miss your bus!
Maria missed the bus for school.

mop

Herb is mopping the kitchen floor. He mopped all the floors.

move

A new family is moving into our building. The other family moved out last week.

Action Words

name

The cowboy is naming the horse.
He named the horse Tim.

need

The plant needs water. It also
needed sunlight.

open

Sally is opening her book.
She opened it to a picture.

own

Jack owns many books. He owned
them for five years.

paint

Jim is painting the fence white.
Someone painted it blue.

Action Words

paste

Wendy is pasting pictures in the book. She pasted many pictures.

patch

Joe is patching his beach ball. He patched it in two places.

pick

Aunt May is picking apples. She picked enough apples to make a pie.

plant

Father is planting trees. He planted two trees in our front yard and two in the back yard.

Action Words

play

Ann is playing the piano. She just
played a new song.

point

Henry is pointing at the blue kite.
Bill pointed at the red kite.

pour

Frank is pouring milk. He poured
a glassful for you.

print

Jim is printing his name again.
He printed it too big.

70

Action Words

pull

The dog was pulling the wagon all day. He pulled it slowly.

push

Dad is pushing the door shut. He pushed it open.

quack

The duck is quacking loudly. It quacked for food.

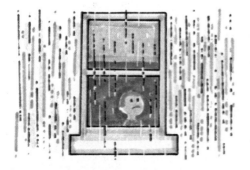

rain

It is raining hard. It rained all afternoon.

Action Words

ride

The dog is riding in the car. It rode to the store. It has ridden many times.

read

Dennis is reading a good story. He read ten books last summer.

rest

Stan is resting in the chair. He rested all afternoon.

roam

The sheep are roaming on the hill. They roamed through a field.

Action Words

rope

The cowboy is roping another calf.
He roped the first calf quickly.

run

Neil is running up the stairs. He
ran down the street fast. He has
run all the way home.

sail

I am sailing a boat.
I sailed on the lake.

saw

Two men are sawing a tree down.
They sawed trees yesterday.

say

Mother was saying no. She said it
to George. She has said it to
George quite often.

Action Words

scare

The noise is scaring the baby. It scared the cat, too.

see

Tony is seeing a movie on TV. He saw it last week, too. He has seen many movies on TV.

sew

Bonny and Dale are sewing their tent. They sewed two torn places.

shake

Don't shake too much pepper on your meat. I shook a lot on mine. Don has shaken salt on his potato.

Action Words

shape

Dan is shaping the clay.
He shaped it into a dog.

shine

The sun is shining on the garden.
It shone brightly in the sky.
The sun shined for three days.

shovel

Frank is shoveling snow. He
shoveled the driveway.

show

Joanne is showing us her frog.
She showed it at school. She has
shown it to everyone.

75

Action Words

sing

Barbara is singing to the baby.
She sang some quiet songs. She has
sung ten songs.

sit

Mother is sitting in the yard.
She sat in the sunshine.

skate

She is skating on the sidewalk.
She skated down a hill.

sleep

The baby is sleeping. He slept
almost all day. He has slept a lot.

Action Words

slide

Fred was sliding on the ice. He slid into a tree. Have you ever slid into a tree?

slither

The snake is slithering in the grass. It slithered under a bush.

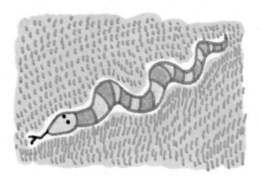

smile

Lin is smiling for her picture. She smiled at the camera.

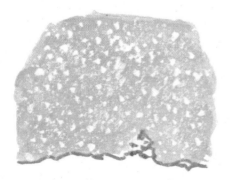

snow

It is snowing again. It snowed all day yesterday.

Action Words

speak

The principal is speaking again. She spoke last week. She has spoken three times.

spill

Henry is spilling the paint. He spilled some of it on the floor.

splash

Dave's dog is splashing water on the floor. He splashed a lot of water on Dave and Julie, too.

spread

Bud is spreading peanut butter on his bread. He spread a lot on one slice. He has spread some for you.

Action Words

squelch

Lois's shoes are squelching in the mud. Her shoes squelched as she walked.

stand

The man is standing in the bus. He stood all the way home. Have you ever stood all the way downtown?

start

The race is starting. Many people started to run.

stay

John is staying at Ray's house. He stayed overnight.

stick

Winnie Mae is sticking pins in the cloth. I stuck pins in some cloth, too. She has stuck her finger!

Action Words

stir

María is stirring the paint. She stirred it to mix it.

stop

Father is stopping the car. He stopped it in the driveway.

sweep

Hank and Heidi are sweeping the garage. They swept the driveway, too. Have they swept the walk yet?

swim

Princess is swimming in the pool. She swam under the diving board. She has swum all around the edge.

Action Words

swing

Karen is swinging in the swing.
She swung high. She has swung
higher than Sue.

take

Wally is taking another snack.
He took one for me. We have taken
only two snacks.

talk

John is talking to Ruth. He talked
about school.

tear

Frisky is tearing paper. He tore
the magazine. He has torn every
magazine in the house.

Action Words

tell

Gail was telling a story. She told the story well. She has told many stories to the class.

thank

Carol is thanking Kathy for the gift. She thanked Kathy for coming to her birthday party.

think

Mr. Lopez is thinking. He thought about which shirt to wear.

throw

Jack was throwing the ball. He threw it to Tom. Tom has thrown the ball in the bushes again.

Action Words

touch

The baby was touching the stuffed bear. He touched it gently.

try

Matt is trying to reach the ball. He tried, but could not reach it.

use

Mother is using the lawnmower. She used it to cut the grass.

wade

Bobby is wading in the pool. He waded there yesterday.

Action Words

walk

Ann is walking to school. She walked home yesterday.

want

Lee wants a new game. She wanted it for a long time.

wash

We are washing the car. We washed it inside and out.

watch

Andy was watching a movie on TV. First he watched a cartoon.

water

Jill is watering her garden. She watered every flower.

Action Words

wear

Sue is wearing her new coat. She wore it to the party. She has worn it twice.

weave

Alice is weaving a basket. She wove part of it in school. She has woven two other baskets.

weigh

Mother is weighing the baby again. She weighed him only yesterday.

whistle

Pete was whistling for the dog. He whistled as loud as he could.

Action Words

wind

Joe is winding the clock. He wound it last week. He hasn't wound it since it stopped.

wink

Father is winking at the baby. The baby winked at me.

wish

Matt is wishing for a new bike. He wished for a yellow bike.

work

Uncle Ben is working in the yard. He worked all day.

wrap

Lucy is wrapping a present. She wrapped it in blue paper.

Action Words

write

Pam is writing her name. She wrote it on paper. She has written it carefully this time.

yawn

The dog is yawning. It yawned all morning. It's a lazy dog.

yell

Sue is yelling at David. She yelled at Earl, too. They ran through her castle.

zip

Bert was zipping his jacket. He zipped it to the top.

Words That Name Things

air

Gene pumped air into the tire.

airplane   airplanes

An airplane is a flying machine.
Airplanes have wings.

alphabet   alphabets

An alphabet is a group of letters.
There are many different alphabets.

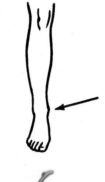

ankle   ankles

Your ankle is between your foot and
your leg.

apple   apples

An apple is a fruit that is good
to eat. Apples grow on trees.

Words That Name Things

arm   arms

Some chairs have arms. You can
rest your arm on the arm of a chair.

armchair   armchairs

An armchair is a kind of chair.
Tom bought two pink armchairs.

back   backs

Your back is the part of your body
opposite the front.

bag   bags

A bag can be made of paper or
cloth. You put things in bags.

balloon   balloons

A balloon is a kind of rubber bag.
You blow air into it.

Words That Name Things

banana   bananas

A banana is a fruit that is good
to eat. Bananas grow on trees.

bank   banks

A bank is a kind of box. You can
put pennies in a bank to save them.

bark

Bark is a part of a tree. It is
on the trunk of a tree.

basket   baskets

A basket holds things. Some
baskets are big. Some are little.

bat   bats

A bat is a long, thin piece of
wood. You hit a ball with a bat.

Words That Name Things

bathtub   bathtubs

You fill a bathtub with water.
Then you sit in it to take a bath.

bean   beans

A bean is a kind of vegetable.
Beans are good to eat.

bed   beds

A bed is a soft place where you
can lie down. You sleep on a bed.

beet   beets

A beet is a kind of vegetable.
Some beets are red.

belt   belts

A belt is a strip of cloth or
leather. You wear a belt around
your waist.

Words That Name Things

bicycle   bicycles

A bicycle has two wheels. You push pedals to make it go.

bike   bikes

Bike is another name for bicycle.

birdhouse   birdhouses

A birdhouse is a small box where birds may live. Some birds make nests in birdhouses.

blanket   blankets

A blanket keeps you warm. Some blankets are soft and fluffy.

birthday   birthdays

A birthday is the day on which a person is born. Birthdays can be happy days.

Words That Name Things

boat   boats

A boat is something to ride in on water. You cross a lake in a boat.

body   bodies

Every person has a body. Animals and fish have bodies, too.

bone   bones

There are many bones in your body. An animal has bones, too.

book   books

A book has sheets of paper inside two covers. Many books have colored pictures.

boot   boots

Boots keep your feet and legs dry. Wear boots when you go out in the snow or rain.

Words That Name Things

bottle   bottles

A bottle can hold milk or juice.
Some bottles are made of glass.

box   boxes

A box holds things. There are all
kinds of boxes. Some are little.

bread

Bread is a kind of food. Bread
with butter on it is good to eat.

breakfast   breakfasts

Breakfast is a kind of meal. Ray
and I ate our breakfasts.

bridge   bridges

A bridge is a road or walk over
water. You can cross a river by
going over a bridge.

Words That Name Things

broom   brooms

A broom is a brush with a long handle. You sweep with a broom.

brush   brushes

A brush is made of stiff hairs or wires. Some brushes are used to clean teeth or to paint houses.

building   buildings

A building has walls and a roof. Schools and houses are buildings.

bunch   bunches

A bunch is a group of things. You can buy flowers in bunches.

bus   buses

A bus is like a large car. Some children ride in school buses.

Words That Name Things

butter

You put butter on bread and toast.

button   buttons

A button is used to hold clothes together. A shirt has buttons down the front.

calendar   calendars

A calendar shows the months, weeks, and days of the year.

can   cans

A can is used to hold something. Many kinds of food are in cans.

Words That Name Things

candle   candles

A candle gives light as it burns.
Birthday cakes often have candles.

cap   caps

A cap is like a hat. You wear
a cap on your head.

capsule   capsules

The capsule is part of a spaceship.
Astronauts ride back to earth in
the capsule.

car   cars

A car is a machine that moves.
People ride in cars.

carrot   carrots

A carrot is a vegetable. Carrots grow under the ground.

cereal   cereals

Cereal is a kind of food. Oatmeal and rice are cereals.

chain   chains

A chain is made of metal rings fastened together.

chair   chairs

You sit on a chair. A chair has a seat and a back.

chalk

Chalk is like a crayon. You write with chalk on a chalkboard.

chalkboard   chalkboards

A chalkboard is on the wall of the schoolroom.

Words That Name Things

chin   chins

Your chin is the part of your face
below your mouth.

class   classes

A class is a group of pupils.
Most schools have many classes.

clock   clocks

A clock shows what time it is.

clothes

People wear clothes. Dresses, pants,
sweaters, and shirts are clothes.
Hats and shoes are clothes, too.

clay

Clay is a kind of wet dirt. You
can shape clay into things.

99

Words That Name Things

cloud   clouds

A cloud often hides the sun in the sky. Some clouds bring rain.

clue   clues

A clue helps you answer a question. The man looked for clues.

coat   coats

A coat keeps you warm when it is cold outside.

comb   combs

Use a comb to keep your hair neat and in place.

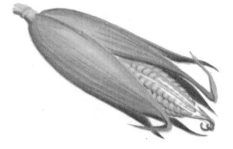

corn

Corn is a vegetable. Animals and people eat corn.

Words That Name Things

costume   costumes

A costume is a kind of clothing. Boys and girls wear costumes on Halloween.

crayon   crayons

Crayons are used for drawing and coloring pictures.

cup   cups

A cup is a dish to drink from. You drink cocoa from a cup.

desk   desks

You write at a desk. Some desks have tops that roll down.

dish   dishes

A dish holds food. Cups and plates are dishes.

Words That Name Things

doll   dolls

A doll is a toy person. Some children like to play with dolls.

door   doors

You open a door to go into a building or a room.

dream   dreams

You may have a dream while you sleep. Dreams can be good or bad.

dress   dresses

A dress is something a girl wears. Dresses are clothes.

drum   drums

A drum makes a loud noise when you hit it.

dryer   dryers

You put clothes in the dryer after they are washed.

Words That Name Things

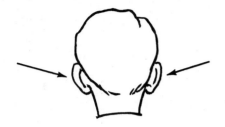

ear   ears

An ear is part of the body. You hear with your ears.

egg   eggs

An egg is good to eat. Some people have eggs for breakfast.

elbow   elbows

Your elbow is the middle part of your arm. You can bend your elbow.

elevator   elevators

An elevator is like a small room that moves. You ride up and down in an elevator.

end

An end is the last part of something. The end of the kite is a tail.

Words That Name Things

escalator   escalators

An escalator is moving stairs.
You go upstairs on an escalator.

eye   eyes

Your eye is in your face. You see
with your eyes.

face   faces

Your face is the front of your
head. Everyone's face is different.

face   faces

The front of a clock is its face.

fan   fans

An electric fan helps keep you cool
in hot weather.

Words That Name Things

feather   feathers

A feather is part of a bird's body.
Feathers are soft and light.

fence   fences

A fence around a garden or yard
keeps animals out.

festival   festivals

A festival is a very large party.
You can have fun at festivals.

finger   fingers

A finger is part of your hand.

fire   fires

A fire is made by burning
something. Fires can be dangerous.

Words That Name Things

fire hydrant   fire hydrants

Water comes from a fire hydrant.
Firemen put out fires with the water.

fire truck   fire trucks

Firemen ride to a fire on a fire
truck. Most fire trucks are red.

flag   flags

The American flag is red, white,
and blue.

flashlight   flashlights

A flashlight is a small light.
It helps you see in the dark.

flower   flowers

A flower grows from a seed or bulb.
Many flowers smell sweet.

Words That Name Things

food   foods

Food is what you eat. Fruits, vegetables, and meats are food.

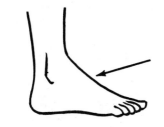

foot   feet

Your foot is at the end of your leg. People have two feet.

football   footballs

A football is a kind of ball. Footballs are fun to play with.

fork   forks

You use a fork to lift food from a dish to your mouth.

fruit   fruits

Apples, oranges, and bananas are kinds of fruit.

Words That Name Things

fun

Fun is a good time. Kim and Ray had fun on the swings.

fur   furs

Fur is the hair that covers many animals.

game   games

A game is something you can play. Children like to play games.

gate   gates

A gate is a door in a wall or fence.

glass   glasses

You can drink water or milk or orange juice from a glass.

Words That Name Things

glove   gloves

You wear a glove on your hand.
Gloves keep your hands warm.

grape   grapes

A grape is a small, round fruit.
Grapes may be red, purple, or green.

grass

Grass grows in fields, in parks, and
in yards.

guitar   guitars

You play a guitar with your fingers.

hair

Hair is what covers your head.
Some people have long hair.

Words That Name Things

hamburger hamburgers

Hamburger is a kind of meat. Most people like to eat a humburger in a bun.

hammer hammers

You use a hammer to pound nails into wood.

hand hands

Your hand is at the end of your arm.

hand hands

The big hand and the little hand of a clock tell the time.

handkerchief handkerchiefs

A handkerchief is a piece of cloth. You use your handkerchief when you blow your nose.

Words That Name Things

hat   hats

You wear a hat on your head.

hay

Hay is grass that is dry. Horses
and cows eat hay.

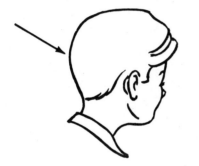

head   heads

Your head is part of your body. It
is above your neck. Hair grows on
your head.

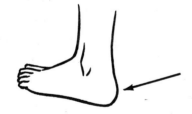

heel   heels

Your heel is the back part of your
foot.

helicopter   helicopters

A helicopter is a flying machine.
It has no wings.

Words That Name Things

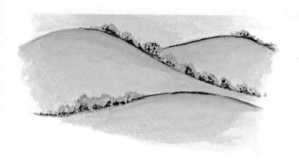

hill   hills

A hill is a part of the earth.
Hills are smaller than mountains.

hoe   hoes

You use a hoe to break up dirt in
a garden or yard.

home   homes

A home is a place where you live.
There are many kinds of homes.

honey

Honey is sweet. Honey tastes good
on toast.

hook   hooks

A hook holds something. Hang
your coat on a hook.

112

Words That Name Things

ice

Ice is frozen water. In winter
there is ice on the pond.

iron   irons

A hot iron makes clothes smooth.

ironing board   ironing boards

You put your clothes on an ironing
board to iron them.

island   islands

An island is land with water all
around it. There are many islands
in the oceans.

jacket   jackets

A jacket is a kind of short coat.
Boys and girls both wear jackets.

Words That Name Things

jacks

Jacks are little pieces of metal.
You play a game with them.

jar   jars

A jar holds things. Some jars are
made of glass.

jeans

Jeans are a kind of pants. Wear
jeans when you work outdoors.

jeep   jeeps

A jeep is a kind of car. Jeeps
can go across fields.

jelly   jellies

Jelly tastes good on toast or bread.

jump rope   jump ropes

You use a jump rope to play a game.
You swing the rope and jump over it.

Words That Name Things

key   keys

A key locks and unlocks doors.
Put keys on a ring so you don't
lose them.

kite   kites

A kite will fly on a windy day.
Sometimes kites get caught in trees.

knee   knees

Your knee is part of your leg.
Your knees bend so you can walk.

knife   knives

You cut your food with a knife.

ladder   ladders

You climb up on a ladder to reach
high places.

Words That Name Things

lake   lakes

A lake is water with land around it. You can swim in lakes.

lamp   lamps

A lamp gives light. You turn on a lamp when it gets dark.

land   lands

Land is another name for ground or soil.

lasso   lassos

A lasso is a rope used by cowboys and cowgirls. Lassos are used to catch horses and cattle.

leaf   leaves

A leaf is part of a tree or plant. Most leaves are green.

leg   legs

Your leg is part of your body. You stand on your legs.

Words That Name Things

letter   letters

The first letter in a person's name is a capital.

light   lights

Cary has a light in his room. There are two lights in the kitchen.

line   lines

A line is a long mark. You can draw lines on paper.

loaf   loaves

A loaf is a large piece of bread. Loaves can be cut into slices.

lunch   lunches

Lunch is a kind of meal. The pupils ate their lunches in school.

lunchtime   lunchtimes

Lunchtime is when you eat lunch.

Words That Name Things

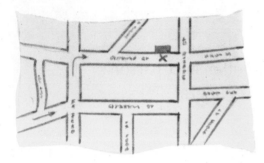

mail

Letters and packages are mail.
Mail carriers bring the mail.

map   maps

A map is a drawing. A map can
help you find your way.

meat   meats

Meat is a kind of food. Meat
comes from animals.

milk

Milk comes from cows. Drinking
milk every day makes you grow.

mitten   mittens

A mitten has a thumb but no
fingers. Mittens keep your hands
warm when it is cold outside.

money

You buy things with money. People
work to get money.

Words That Name Things

moon

The moon is bright in the sky at night. A full moon is round.

mop   mops

You can use a mop to clean the floor. A mop has a long handle.

mouth   mouths

Your mouth is in your head. You eat and talk with your mouth.

movie   movies

A movie tells a story with pictures. Some movies are funny.

mustard

You can put mustard on a sandwich. Mustard is yellow.

Words That Name Things

nail   nails

A nail holds pieces of wood together. You pound nails with a hammer.

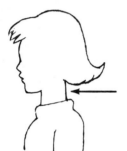

name   names

Everyone has a name. Some names are short.

neck   necks

Your neck is the part of your body between your head and shoulders.

nest   nests

A nest is the kind of home birds build. Baby birds live in nests.

newspaper   newspapers

A newspaper tells what is happening. People read newspapers every day.

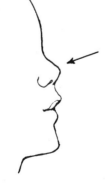

nose   noses

Your nose is part of your face. You can smell things with your nose.

Words That Name Things

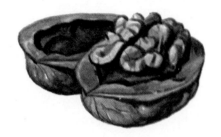

number   numbers

A number is a word that tells how many. You use numbers in math.

nut   nuts

A nut grows on a tree. Some nuts are good to eat.

oat   oats

An oat is a kind of plant. Oatmeal is made from oats.

orange   oranges

An orange is a fruit. Oranges grow on trees. Orange juice is good to drink.

oven   ovens

An oven is a place for baking food. Some kitchens have two ovens.

Words That Name Things

pan   pans

A pan is a dish you cook food in.

pants

Many people wear pants. Some pants are long. Some are short.

paper   papers

You can write on paper. You can wrap something in paper, too.

part   parts

A part is a thing that helps make up something. A puzzle has many parts.

paste

Paste makes pieces of paper stick together.

Words That Name Things

peanut   peanuts

A peanut is a kind of seed that is good to eat. Peanuts are used to make peanut butter.

pear   pears

A pear is a fruit. Pears grow on trees.

pen   pens

You can write on paper with a pen. A pen has ink in it.

pencil   pencils

You write with a pencil. A pencil must have a sharp point.

piano   pianos

Some people can play music on a piano. Some people can't.

Words That Name Things

pickle   pickles

A pickle tastes sour or sweet.
Most pickles are green.

picnic   picnics

A picnic is a party with a meal
outdoors. People go on picnics
in the summer.

picture   pictures

You can draw a picture or paint
a picture.

piece   pieces

A piece is one part of a thing.
A puzzle may have many pieces.

pillow   pillows

A pillow is soft. Put your head
on the pillow and go to sleep.

pitcher   pitchers

You can pour milk from a pitcher
into a glass.

Words That Name Things

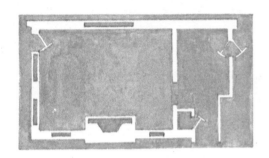

plan   plans

A plan shows how to do something. Plans are used to build homes.

plane   planes

A plane is an airplane.

plant   plants

A plant grows in the ground. Trees are plants.

plate   plates

A plate is a flat dish.

popcorn

Popcorn is fun to pop and good to eat. Put salt and butter on it.

potato   potatoes

A potato is a vegetable. Sweet potatoes are yellow.

Words That Name Things

puppet   puppets

You put a puppet over your hand.
Your fingers make it move.

purse   purses

You carry things in a purse.

puzzle   puzzles

A puzzle is a kind of game. Some
puzzles are hard.

quill   quills

A quill is a stiff, sharp hair.
A porcupine is covered with quills.

radio   radios

You can hear music on a radio.

rain

Rain is drops of water falling
from clouds.

Words That Name Things

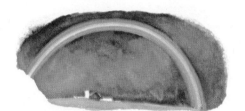

rainbow   **rainbows**

A rainbow has many colors. You see rainbows in the sky.

raincoat   **raincoats**

A raincoat helps keep you dry on a rainy day.

record player   **record players**

You play records on a record player. There are two record players in our school.

refrigerator   **refrigerators**

A refrigerator is cold inside. You keep food in it.

road   **roads**

A road is a kind of street. You travel on roads to get somewhere.

Words That Name Things

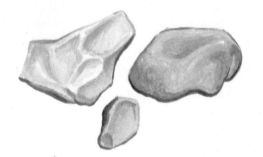

rock   rocks

A rock is a large stone. Rocks are hard and heavy.

room   rooms

A room is part of a building. This room is a kitchen.

root   roots

A root is part of a plant. Roots grow under the ground.

roundup   roundups

Cowboys and cowgirls work in a roundup. Roundups bring animals together.

salad   salads

A salad can be different vegetables served with a dressing. Salads are good to eat.

sand

Sand feels like sugar or salt.
Sand is not good to eat.

sandbox   sandboxes

A sandbox is a big box filled with
sand. Children play in sandboxes.

sandwich   sandwiches

A sandwich is two pieces of bread
with something in between them.

satellite   satellites

A satellite looks like a star. It
moves in the sky.

saucer   saucers

A saucer is a small flat dish.
You set a cup on a saucer.

Words That Name Things

saw   saws

You can cut wood with a saw.

scarf   scarves

You wear a scarf around your neck or on your head. Al has two scarves.

scissors

You can cut paper with scissors.

secret   secrets

A secret is something you don't tell anyone. Can you keep secrets?

seed   seeds

If you plant a seed in the ground, it will grow.

seesaw   seesaws

It is fun to ride on a seesaw.

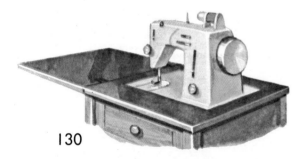

sewing machine   sewing machines

A person can make clothes with a sewing machine.

Words That Name Things

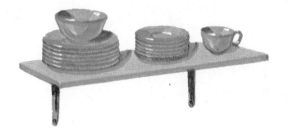

shelf   shelves

There is a shelf for the dishes.
Are there any shelves for the
books and records?

shell   shells

A shell is a hard covering. Nuts
have shells.

ship   ships

A ship is a large boat. Ships
cross the ocean.

shirt   shirts

A boy or a girl may wear a shirt.
Some shirts have long sleeves.

shoe   shoes

A shoe is worn on a foot. Don't
wear shoes that are too short.

Words That Name Things

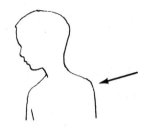

shoulder   shoulders

Your shoulder is between your neck and your arm.

shovel   shovels

You can pick up dirt or snow with a shovel. Power shovels are big digging machines.

sidewalk   sidewalks

Walk on the sidewalk. That's what sidewalks are for.

sink   sinks

You can wash dishes or get a drink of water at the sink.

skate   skates

A skate fits on your foot. You can go over ice with ice skates on. Roller skates have wheels.

Words That Name Things

skirt   skirts

A skirt is something a girl can wear with a blouse or a shirt.

smoke

Smoke is the gas and ash that comes from a fire.

slacks

Slacks are a kind of pants. Both boys and girls wear slacks.

slide   slides

There is a slide on the playground. It is fun to go down a slide.

snow

Snow falls in tiny white flakes.

sound   sounds

A sound is something you can hear. You can hear the sounds of a horn.

sock   socks

A sock covers your foot. Be sure both socks are the same color.

Words That Name Things

soup   soups

Soup is a kind of food. You eat soup with a spoon.

spaceship   spaceships

A spaceship can travel to other planets. Spaceships are used to explore outer space.

spoon   spoons

You eat ice cream and soup with a spoon. Some spoons are big.

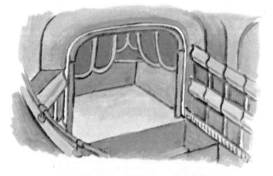

stable   stables

A stable is a building where horses or cattle are kept. Most farms have stables.

stage   stages

A stage is a part of a theater. Plays are performed on stages.

star   stars

A star is far away. There are many stars in the sky at night.

Words That Name Things

stem   stems

A stem is part of a plant. This rose has a long stem.

step   steps

A step is something you walk on to go up or down. Let's sit on the front steps for a while.

stick   sticks

A stick is a long, thin piece of wood. Throw a stick on the fire.

stone   stones

A stone is hard. Stones on the beach hurt your feet.

stool   stools

A stool is like a chair with no back or arms.

Words That Name Things

stop sign   stop signs

A stop sign is red. Cars must stop at a stop sign.

stove   stoves

You can cook food on a stove.

street cleaner   street cleaners

A street cleaner is a big machine that cleans the streets.

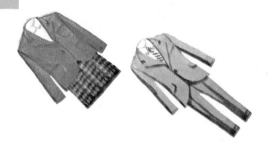

string   strings

A string is a very thin rope.
I used two strings to tie the box.

suit   suits

A girl's suit may have a skirt and a jacket or pants and a jacket. A boy's suit has pants and a jacket.

sun

The sun makes the light every day.

Words That Name Things

sweater   sweaters

You can wear a sweater with pants or a skirt. Sweaters keep you warm.

swing   swings

A swing moves back and forth. There are swings on our playground.

table   tables

A table has legs and a flat top. You can put things on a table.

taco   tacos

A taco is a kind of food. You can buy tacos at a taco stand.

tail   tails

A tail is part of an animal's body.

taxicab   taxicabs

A taxicab is a car. You have to pay when you ride in it.

Words That Name Things

teeth

You bite and chew with your teeth.
Each one of your teeth is a tooth.

telephone   telephones

You can talk into a telephone and
hear someone answer.

television   televisions

Do you like to watch television?
We have two televisions at home.

thermometer   thermometers

A thermometer can tell you if
you have a fever. Doctors and
nurses use thermometers.

thing   things

What one thing would you like to
have? Please put your things away.

thread

You sew clothes with thread.

Words That Name Things

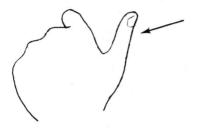

thumb   thumbs

Your thumb is the short, thick
finger of your hand.

tie   ties

You wear a tie around your neck.
Some ties are brightly colored.

time

What time is it? It is time
to go home.

tire   tires

A tire fits on the edge of a wheel.
Tires are filled with air.

toast

Toast is bread that has been
toasted until it is brown.

toaster   toasters

You put bread in a toaster to
make toast.

Words That Name Things

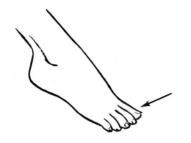

toe   toes

A toe is on the end of your foot.
People have five toes on each foot.

tooth   teeth

A tooth is one of your teeth.

toothpick   toothpicks

A toothpick is a small, pointed
piece of wood. Toothpicks can
be used for many things.

top   tops

A top is a toy that spins. Some
tops make a noise.

tortilla   tortillas

A tortilla is a round, thin cake.

toy   toys

A toy is something to play with.
Dolls, balls, jacks, tops, and
kites are toys.

Words That Name Things

traffic light   traffic lights

A traffic light tells you when to
cross the street.

trail   trails

A trail is a kind of path.
You can hike on trails.

train   trains

A train has many cars hooked
together. Trains run on a track.

treasure   treasures

Treasure is something of great
value. A pirate's chest may be
filled with treasures.

tree   trees

A tree has a trunk, branches, and
leaves. There are many different
kinds of trees.

Words That Name Things

truck   trucks

A truck is a kind of car. Trucks carry heavy loads.

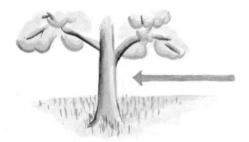

trunk   trunks

A trunk is a part of a tree. Trees have bark on their trunks.

umbrella   umbrellas

An umbrella keeps the rain off your head.

vacuum cleaner   vacuum cleaners

A vacuum cleaner cleans rugs. It cleans floors and furniture, too.

vegetable   vegetables

A vegetable is a kind of food that grows as a plant. Peas and potatoes and beans are vegetables.

Words That Name Things

vine   vines

A vine is a plant that grows along the ground. Some vines grow up on walls and fences.

wagon   wagons

You can put groceries in a wagon and pull it home.

wall   walls

A wall is the side of a house or room. Joy will paint the walls.

washer   washers

Throw all your dirty clothes in the washer.

watch   watches

A watch is a clock you can wear on your wrist.

water

You can drink water. You can wash your face in water.

Words That Name Things

weather

The weather is sunny and warm.

web   webs

A web is a spider's home. Most spiders spin webs.

wheel   wheels

A wheel is round. Cars have four wheels. Bicycles have two.

window   windows

A window is an open place in a wall. Houses have windows.

wing   wings

A wing is part of a bird. Birds can't fly without wings.

word   words

A word is a group of sounds that has a meaning. You use words to make sentences.

Words That Name Things

wrist   wrists

Your wrist is between your arm
and your hand.

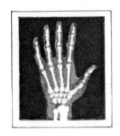

X ray   X rays

An X ray of your hand will show
the bones.

yarn

Yarn is like thread. You make
sweaters out of yarn.

yo-yo   yo-yos

A yo-yo is a toy. It moves up
and down on a string.

zipper   zippers

A jacket may have a zipper
instead of buttons.

Words That Name Places

airport   airports

Airplanes land and take off from an airport.

apartment building apartment buildings

A big apartment building has many families living in it.

aquarium   aquariums

You can see many kinds of fish at an aquarium.

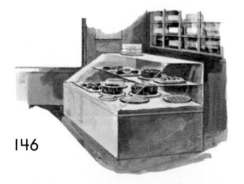

bakery   bakeries

You can buy bread at a bakery.
Bakers work in bakeries.

Words That Name Places

beach   beaches

A beach is a strip of land next to the water. Some beaches are sandy.

bus station   bus stations

People wait for a bus at the bus station.

cafeteria   cafeterias

You eat at a cafeteria. You carry your food on a tray.

camp   camps

People who go to camp sometimes sleep in tents.

castle   castles

A castle has walls around it. In stories kings live in castles.

147

Words That Name Places

center   centers

A neighborhood center is a good place to play games.

church   churches

Some people go to a church to worship and pray.

city   cities

Many people live in a city. Most cities have big buildings.

corner   corners

Two streets meet at a corner. Wait for your bus at the corner.

country

Country is the land outside a city. Farms are in the country.

148

Words That Name Places

den   dens

A den is an animal's home. Bear cubs live in dens.

drugstore   drugstores

You buy medicine at a drugstore.

dump   dumps

A dump is a place to throw things you don't want any longer.

earth

The earth is a huge planet. It has mountains and oceans and rivers. All the people and animals live on the earth.

factory   factories

People make things at a factory. TV sets are made in factories.

149

Words That Name Places

fairground   fairgrounds
You go to the fairground to see the fair.

farm   farms
A farmer raises animals and food on a farm.

field   fields
A field is part of a farm. Corn grows in fields.

firehouse   firehouses
Fire trucks are kept in a firehouse.

garage   garages
Cars are kept or fixed at a garage. Mechanics fix cars in garages.

Words That Name Places

garden   gardens

You can grow vegetables and flowers in a garden.

gas station   gas stations

Drivers buy gas at a gas station.

harbor   harbors

A harbor is a safe place for boats to stay.

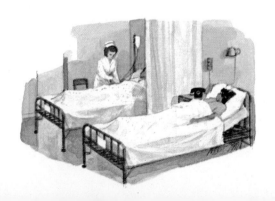

hospital   hospitals

A hospital is a good place for sick people. They are cared for at a hospital.

Words That Name Places

hotel   hotels

A hotel has rooms for people to sleep in. People pay to stay overnight in a hotel.

house   houses

A house is a building for people to live in.

library   libraries

Books are kept in a library. You can borrow books at most libraries.

moon

The moon is a satellite.
It moves around the earth.
Astronauts have been to the moon.

Words That Name Places

mosque   mosques

Some people go to a mosque to worship and pray.

motel   motels

People can stay overnight at a motel when they take a long trip.

mountain   mountains

A mountain is a very high hill. Some mountains have snow on top even in summer.

museum   museums

You can see dinosaur bones at a museum. You can see stuffed animals and stuffed birds, too.

Words That Name Places

neighborhood   neighborhoods

A neighborhood is the part of town where you live. There is a drugstore in our neighborhood.

observatory   observatories

At an observatory scientists watch the stars move.

office   offices

People work in an office.

palace   palaces

A king or queen lives in a palace. Palaces are huge houses with beautiful gardens and trees.

Words That Name Places

park   parks

A park has grass and trees. Let's have a picnic in the park.

parking lot   parking lots

A parking lot is a place to park many cars.

place   places

What is the most interesting place you have ever seen? There are many places to see in the city.

playground   playgrounds

You go to the playground to play. Some playgrounds have swings and slides and merry-go-rounds.

155

Words That Name Places

post office   post offices

You can mail a letter at a post office. Mail carriers bring mail to you from the post office.

ranch   ranches

A ranch is a kind of farm where cattle or sheep are raised.

restaurant   restaurants

It is fun to eat at a restaurant. You pay for the food. You eat anything you want.

156

Words That Name Places

school   schools

Children go to school to learn.

sea   seas

A sea is a large body of water.

shop   shops

A shop is a kind of store. You
buy gifts at a gift shop.

shopping center   shopping centers

There are many stores in a big
shopping center.

skating rink   skating rinks

You see some good skaters at a
skating rink.

Words That Name Places

sky   skies

The sky is the air above us. Some skies look very blue.

space   spaces

There is space between the earth and the moon. Astronauts go into space to get to the moon.

store   stores

You buy things in a store. There are many kinds of stores.

street   streets

Our town has one main street. Big cities have many streets. What street does he live on?

Words That Name Places

supermarket   supermarkets

A supermarket is a large store.
You choose what you want to buy.

swimming pool   swimming pools

A swimming pool is a place to
swim. Some swimming pools are
outdoors. Some are indoors.

synagogue   synagogues

Some people go to a synagogue
to worship and pray.

159

Words That Name Places

theater   theaters

You can see a movie or a play at a theater. Our town has a theater and a drive-in movie.

town   towns

A town is a small city.

valley   valleys

The place between two mountains or hills is called a valley.

village   villages

A village is a small town. There are only a few houses in a village.

Words That Name Places

woods

Trees grow close together in the woods. You can get lost there.

world

The world is the earth and everything on it.

yard   yards

A yard is the land and space around a house. Many people plant flowers and grass in their yards.

zoo   zoos

Wild animals are kept at a zoo. You go to the zoo to see them.

Words That Help
Words that tell what kind

The angry man looked at the window.

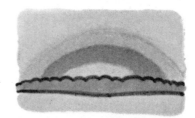

We saw a beautiful rainbow today.
It is the best rainbow I have seen.
Have you ever seen a better rainbow?

Jerry has a big dog.

Mom is proud of her clean car.

Wear a lot of clothes on a cold day.
Monday was a colder day than today.
Tomorrow may be the coldest day.

Words that tell what kind

It's spooky on a dark night.

Kenji owns many different shirts.

The funny clown made us laugh.
We were glad to see him.
The clown did a good trick.
We had a great time!

Marcia is sewing a handmade quilt.

The happy girl got a pair of skates.

Words that tell what kind

We may have hot weather in July.
The fourth of July is an important day.

The kind boy helped Mr. Winters.

Ida is carrying a large picture.

Do you like my new leather boots?

A little kangaroo is easy to carry.

Words that tell what kind

This sweater has long sleeves.

We have new kittens at home.

The old man was sitting in the sun.

The plump chicks followed the hen.

I bought a pretty yellow rose.

Words that tell what kind

We saw a sad movie on TV.
Would you see it a second time?

This pencil has a sharp point.

Laurie slipped on the slick ice.

The slow turtle lost the race.

Chris's sweater has a small hole.

Words that tell what kind

Kay gave me a special valentine.

The boat was tossed in the stormy lake.

A tall person can see a lot.

Greg wore an ugly Halloween mask.

Wear only a few clothes on a warm day.
Sunday was a warmer day than today.
Friday may be the warmest day of the year.

Words that tell what color

black

blue

brown

gray

green

lavender

orange

pink

purple

red

white

yellow

Words that tell how much or how many

a few peanuts

lots of peanuts

many peanuts

a little snow   a lot of snow

All the children are smiling.   an empty basket

None of the children are smiling.   a full basket

Words that tell how much or how many

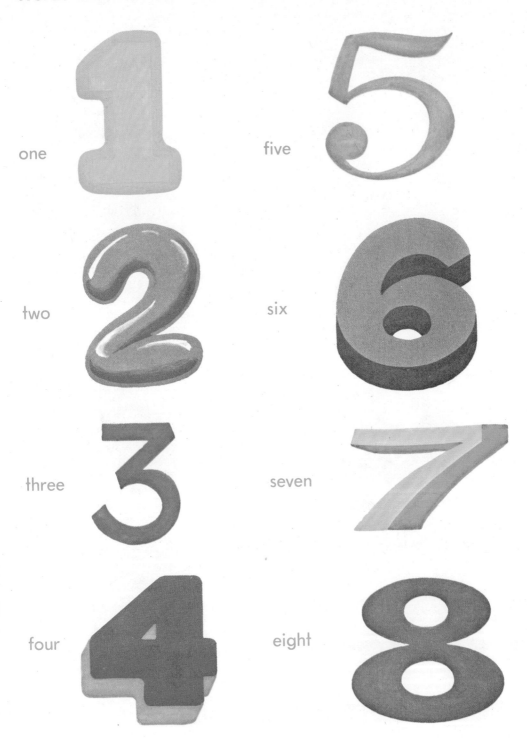

one

two

three

four

five

six

seven

eight

Words that tell how much or how many

nine **9**

ten **10**

eleven **11**

twelve **12**

penny
cent

nickel

dime

quarter

dollar

Words that tell how

He skates badly.

The sun shone brightly.

He wrote his name carefully.

She wrote her name carelessly.

Racing cars go fast.

Words that tell how

He hit the ball hard.

She sadly waved good-by.

He ate his ice-cream cone slowly.

The horse stopped suddenly.

They do their work well.

Words that tell when

before

after

early

late

always

never

Words that tell when

yesterday

today

tomorrow

morning

afternoon

evening

day

night

Words that tell when

Words that tell when

January

February

March   spring

April

May

June   summer

July

August

                                                     fall

September   autumn

October

November

                                                   winter

December

Words that tell where

The flag is above the school.

The playground is by the school.

A slide is across from the swings.

A boy is ahead of the girl.

A fence is around the playground.

Words that tell where

A boy is at the chalkboard.

The teacher is behind her desk.

A bookcase is below the windows.

A girl is beside the bookcase.

179

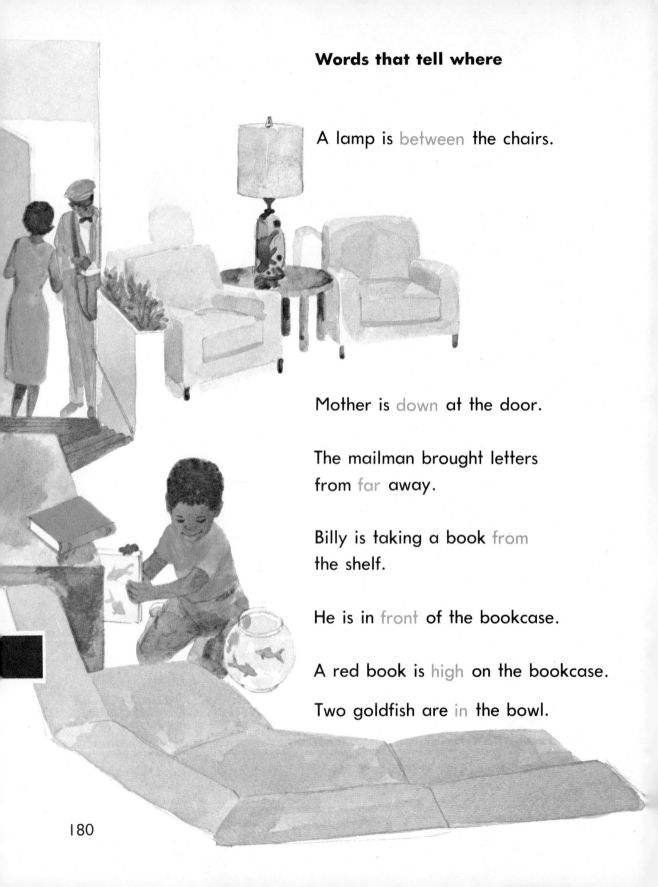

Words that tell where

A lamp is between the chairs.

Mother is down at the door.

The mailman brought letters
from far away.

Billy is taking a book from
the shelf.

He is in front of the bookcase.

A red book is high on the bookcase.

Two goldfish are in the bowl.

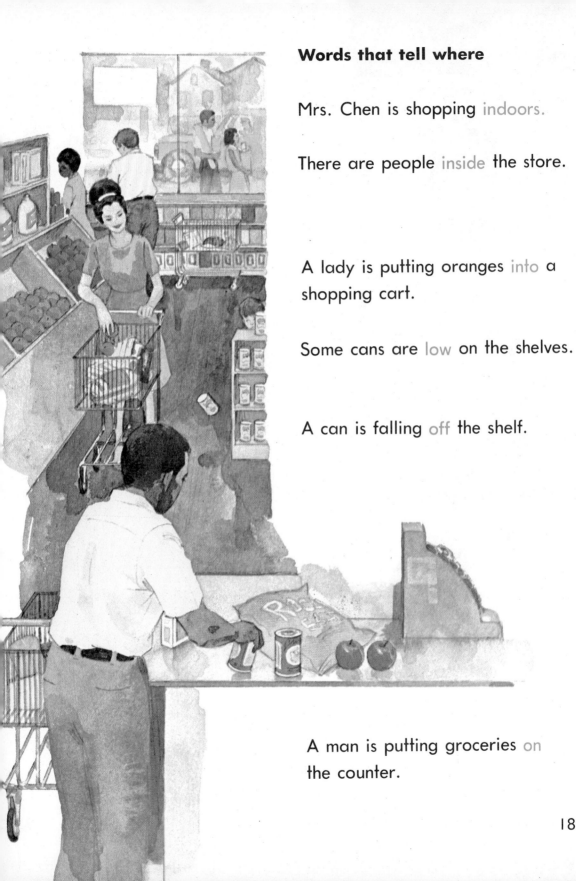

Words that tell where

Mrs. Chen is shopping indoors.

There are people inside the store.

A lady is putting oranges into a shopping cart.

Some cans are low on the shelves.

A can is falling off the shelf.

A man is putting groceries on the counter.

Words that tell where

The boy is running out the door.

He wants to play outdoors.

His friends are outside the house.

One boy is jumping over a puddle on the sidewalk.

They are going to the park.

Lee and Ken are playing upstairs.

The canary is up in the cage.

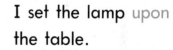

I set the lamp upon
the table.

The dog is sleeping
under the chair.

The basement is underneath
the house.

Words that tell which one

Ann took the first seat in the row.

No one took the next seat in the row.

Danny took the last seat in the row.

The pencil is in Lucy's left hand.

Eric is standing on his right foot.

That book is the one I want.

Manuel read these books.

Would this book do?

Index

D'Nealian Alphabet

0 1 2 3 4 5 6

7 8 9 10 a b c

d e f g h i j

k l m n o p q

r s t u v w x

y z A B C D E

F G H I J K L

M N O P Q R S

T U V W X Y Z